OFF THE SHELF

Serving God in the Senior Years

Frank Gillham

Contents

Preface

The number of people over sixty-five years old increases each year. However, our world is geared toward emphasizing youthfulness. When I was younger, we depended on the daily paper as our news source. One of the most popular sections was the "funnies." Characters such as "Mutt and Jeff" and "Blondie and Dagwood" always brought a chuckle. Today, we have television "funnies." Much of what we see is information about our world in general. While it is helpful, most of what is called news focuses on war, murder, rape, and dishonest news centered in the political arena. Have you noticed that most of the media focus on youth in presenting the daily news? A well-coiffed young person with an ear-to-ear smile will share the "news" whether it be good, bad, or ugly. Where are the Walter Cronkite and Barbara Walters of our world today?

The purpose of writing *Off The Shelf* is twofold. We hope to encourage young people to see the value of older people and, we hope to encourage "oldies" to get off the shelf and continue to contribute to our world.

Frank Gillham

Introduction

Off The Shelf, is about life in the senior years. Our own expectations and that of society are that in the retirement years, people will step back from much of their activity, leaving work to the younger ones and enjoy quiet relaxation. Is this the way it should be? Such a view ignores the fact that seniors with their expertise, experience, wisdom, and talents are extremely resourceful, with much to contribute to life in general, and to the Kingdom of God in particular.

Children of God never really retire, do they? In the Scriptures, we see that God did not call only the young to do assignments for him. I like to remember that Moses was 80 years old before he embarked on what could be called his life's work.

My own father lived to be 101 years old and was busy until a month before his death, writing a book that God had instructed him to write.

This book is an attempt to reorient our thinking about senior years. It shares the experiences of many seniors who have refused to stay 'on the shelf' but are actively engaged in life, using their experience, gifts, talents and interests for the greater good.

The Bible says in Psalm 92:13-15:

The righteous will flourish like a palm tree,
 they will grow like a cedar of Lebanon;
planted in the house of the Lord,
 they will flourish in the courts of our God.
They will still bear fruit in old age,
 they will stay fresh and green, proclaiming, "The Lord is
upright; he is my Rock, and there is
no wickedness in him.

Fruitfulness. This is what God helps us to achieve in all stages of life. He chose us that "we should bear fruit and that our fruit should remain" (John 15:16).

It is exciting to see the paths that God will lead us to take in our senior years. In this book, you will see examples of this as persons share their experiences of being off the shelf. May it energize and inspire you.

Dahlia Fraser
Founding Partner, The Well

Section 1

Living Off the Shelf

x

x

Living Off the Shelf

Webster's dictionary: *On the shelf: Out of use, activity, or circulation.*

Recently, I was shopping at the local Sam's Club and as I was leaving, I got into an interesting conversation with the door monitor. He was an older gentleman, nicely dressed and seemingly desirous of conversation. During our chat, He recited the following account: "I had a lengthy service with a well-known community organization and became the President of the company. When I reached birthday number seventy, the board of directors informed me that I had reached retirement age. They reiterated my retirement benefits, gave a lavish dinner for my wife and me, and presented me with a traditional gold watch. The meeting was closed with their singing "For He's a Jolly Good Fellow," warm handshakes and that was it. I was retired. WOW!"

He continued with his story. He said that he and his wife did some very interesting travel, had pleasant unhurried visits with family, and settled into the golden age of being retired. After a year of being a disconnected lazy person, he said that he realized that there must be more to life than tending a small yard and attending church on Sunday mornings. He put his resume out for prospective employment. After numerous meetings with prospective employers, he noted what was becoming a repeated response. All were impressed with his skills but seemed to voice the same concern that his age was a factor. He said that Sam's Club had welcomed him and given him the position of door greeter. His job was to welcome new shoppers, thank those who were finished with their shopping, and see to it that all incoming shoppers had a shopping basket.

I asked this former company president how he felt about being a door greeter. His answer expresses his feelings "Man, I am happy being a door greeter. It means that I'm no longer on the shelf."

I can relate to that scenario. In fact, the growing number of "oldies" can relate. It has become common to refer to us as "on the shelf."

Allow me to get up close and personal. As I write this, I am halfway through my ninety-second year. My purpose is not to draw attention to myself. My wonderful wife, Ann, ascended to her Heavenly home three years ago. She had reached her 87th year. Cancer had taken its toll. After a period of intense grieving, I realized that sweet Ann had gone, more alive than ever, to be in the place prepared. I have many pleasant memories. I was privileged to hold her hand as her labored breathing ceased. Ann's beautiful body had died. Her spirit is more alive than ever. She was ushered into her Heavenly home prepared by our Lord Jesus. As the Apostle Paul said in 1 Corinthians 13:12 "For now we see through a mirror, dimly, but then face to face." I am seeing through a mirror, dimly. Ann is face to face with Christ our Savior. God, in His time, will call me Home. I will see Jesus and the heavenly hosts. I will see Ann.

In the meantime, I must avoid spending the rest of my life on "the shelf." Onward!

Those of us who remain are here for a purpose. While I cherish precious memories, I must follow the example of the Apostle Paul when he said, in Philippians 3:12-13:

> Not that I have already attained this—that is, I have not already been perfected—but I strive to lay hold of that for which Christ Jesus also laid hold of me. Brothers and sisters, I do not consider myself to have attained this. Instead, I am single-minded: Forgetting the things that are behind and reaching out for the things that are ahead, I press toward the goal for the prize of the upward call of God in Christ Jesus.

General "Chinese" Gordon was leading his British forces in Sudan. He assigned one of his officers the task of capturing a strong fortress. After days of hard and demanding conflict, the officer returned to headquarters. Galloping into camp, he reined in his tired steed before General Gordon, saluted, and announced,

"General, I have taken the fort!" His commander calmly replied, "Go take another!"

Make Up Your Mind

In the book *The Vance Havner Devotional Treasury*, the author wrote, "I shall never forget Dr. R. A. Torrey saying to me as a young preacher, 'Young man, make up your mind on one thing and stick to it.'" Havner comments, "The Christian life should be like a sword with one point, not like a broom ending in many straws. Such a single purpose forgets the past, reaches toward the future, and presses on. There is no time or place for side issues, diversions to the right or to the left. There is no place for hands on the plow with eyes looking back. Paul was a one-track man, but you can go a long way on one track!"

Life is really about time –today.

Herr Tevya in "Fiddler on the Roof" expresses

> Is this the little girl I carried?
> Is this the little boy at play?
> I don't remember growing older,
> When did they?
> When did she get to be a beauty?
> When did he grow to be so tall?
> Wasn't it yesterday when they were small
> Sunrise, sunset. Sunrise, sunset,
> Swiftly flow the days.
> Seedlings turn overnight to sunflowers,

Blossoming even as we gaze.
Sunrise, sunset. Sunrise sunset,
swiftly fly the years.
One season following another,
Laden with happiness and tears.

Yesterday is past. Tomorrow has not come. When, and if, tomorrow comes, it will be today. Our focus is to be about today. However, much of what we do today is influenced by what resides in our memory bank. Our memory can serve as a springboard.

Let me illustrate. Early in the summer of 2022, I was whiling away the afternoon and my memory train took me back to 1972. Ann and I were serving in a church in Florida. During that time our church established a mission relationship with the Ocho Rios Baptist Church in Jamaica. Their pastor, Rev. A. Oliver Fraser, became a dear friend, counselor, and co-worker.

Through the miracle of the cell phone, I established contact with the pleasant receptionist at the church. She asked if I had spoken with Reverend Fraser and gave me his phone number. I called immediately and the phone was answered by a pleasant lady. She identified herself as Rev. Fraser's daughter, Dahlia Fraser. She put her dad on the phone. During our conversation, Rev. Fraser shared that he was one hundred and one years old. He revealed that the one more thing he hoped to do was to write and publish his memoirs. Dahlia wrote the book for her father. She is a professionally trained writer and Bible teacher and did a stellar job writing this book for her dad.

His book, *What A God! Reflections of a Centenarian,* has been published and circulated among Christians in Jamacia. Rev. Fraser went Home to our Lord two weeks after he received his book. Trace this story back to memory serving as a springboard. Memory can keep us off the Shelf if we allow it to become a springboard. We profit when we allow our memories to spring us into an effective day.

Adjust and Keep Going

Let's realize. As we become older, we can no longer do what we used to do. That being so, we can be content with what we can do. I remember when I was a young consultant that one day I had a breakfast meeting with a church committee in Fort Lauderdale, Florida, met at the airport in Atlanta, Georgia at noon time, with a group from a church and, addressed the stewardship council of a church in Portland, Oregon that evening. I can no longer do that. I know that. And I must be willing to accept that.

When I was thirty-two years old, living in Japan where my family and I were serving as missionaries, I decided to climb Mount Fuji which is 12,388 feet high. That's quite a climb. It took everything I had to climb the mountain. I cannot even imagine doing that now.

Set smaller goals. I can no longer climb a mountain, however, I can walk around the block.

I think back to some wonderful friends, Jess and Opal Henderson. Jess was a deacon in the First Baptist Church in Dallas, Texas, and a very well-retired businessman. Both are in their Eternal home with our Lord. One day, I asked Jess how it felt to be retired after a successful career in the oil business. He looked up from his wheelchair and said,

"When your mind makes a contract that your body cannot fulfill, then you know, my brother, that you are over the hill. Opal and I asked our Lord to show us what we can do each day."

There are some things that we always need to remember. And that is, we cannot always do what we always did. Nevertheless, that is no excuse for doing nothing. Being placed on the shelf is not inevitable. It is up to each of us to desire that we, personally, are not on "the shelf."

No longer needed

The people around you may be comfortable with your being on the shelf. However, "oldies" are wise to remember to continue to do the best they can with what they have for Jesus' sake today.

I am amazed that those of us who have achieved the status of being old folks are no longer sought for our services. The general public seems happy enough for us to be ensconced on the shelf. Looking back, I must admit that I often failed to avail myself of the services of capable, experienced "oldies." Perhaps I felt threatened.

 It is true that we oldies need to practice discretion and listening. It is good at any age to practice the "Seventy-Thirty" rule, i.e., listen seventy percent of the time and talk thirty percent of the time. A few years ago, I was on a short business trip. As I was returning, I stopped by the office to check my mail. Neatly framed and hanging on my wall were these words: "Franklin, Your ears will not get you in trouble." Ann.

This reminder sits on my desk today. Thanks, I needed that. Unless you have learned everything there is to learn, which you have not, then listen.

It was mid-February 1988. We were in New York over the weekend. The weather was frightful. Snow and sleet were falling in the sub-freezing temperature. The cab driver took us to the Marble Collegiate Church. We doubted anyone would be there on this bad weather day. We were in for a surprise. As we stepped out of the cab in front of the church, two ushers came through the door to welcome us. They said that we were very fortunate because two people had just left and we could have their seats. Otherwise, we would have had to join the more than two hundred folks in the basement overflow auditorium. They told us that the crowd was large because their former pastor, Dr. Norman Vincent Peale, was going to preach the morning sermon. Dr. Peale had become known through his International best-selling book, *The Power of Positive Thinking*. Dr. Peale, a cane in one hand and his Bible in the other mounted the pulpit and preached a spellbinding sermon You are probably wondering what was so unusual about that. Dr. Peale was ninety years old. He continued to serve the Lord for two more years when the Lord called him home.

It reminds us of a well-known hymn: "Oh, Land of Rest, for Thee, I sigh when will the moment come when I shall lay my armor by and reach my Heavenly home? We'll work until Jesus comes and we'll be gathered Home."

> Even youths grow tired and weary, and young men stumble and fall; but those who hope in the LORD will renew their strength. They will soar on wings like eagles; they will run and not grow weary; they will walk and not faint. Isaiah 40:31-32

Attitude matters

Our personal attitudes serve to help us chart our course as we determine to stay off the shelf. Proverbs 23:7 speaks to our attitude. "As a man thinketh in his heart, so is he."

Nineteen years ago, I stepped onto the elevator in a downtown office building in Dallas. The only other person on the elevator was an older gentleman. He had a walking cane in each hand, and he was bent double. He looked up at me and smiled. He said, "I am ninety-six. How old are you?" I replied that I was seventy-two. He replied, "Go for it, Sonny. The world is your oyster. Don't quit." Good advice.

A present-day television advertisement shows a nicely dressed older lady. She is seated and looks up and states, "Age is just a number and mine is unlisted."

Woe to the individual who reminds folks of his/her age constantly. Remember, your attitude determines your altitude.

The promises of God are the perfect guide for our thinking and will help us escape the pitfalls. the Bible is replete with promises God has made to you. And He has a perfect record of keeping all His promises. Here are just five promises from God that you can claim as your very own:

To answer your prayers – Matthew 7:7, "Ask, and it will be given to you; seek, and you will find; knock, and it will be opened to you."

To always be with you – Romans 8:38-39, "For I am persuaded that neither death nor life, nor angels nor principalities nor powers, nor things present nor things to come, nor height nor depth, nor any other created thing, shall be able to separate us from the love of God which is in Christ Jesus our Lord.

To work all things for your good – Romans 8:28, "And we know that all things work together for good to those who love God, to those who are the called according to His purpose."

To take care of all your needs – Philippians 4:19, "And my God shall supply all your needs according to His riches in glory by Christ Jesus."

Freedom from your sin – I John 1:9, "If we confess our sins, He is faithful and just to forgive us our sins and to cleanse us from all unrighteousness."

Navigating your new life

The new retirement lifestyle may be difficult to navigate at first.

You have likely thought a lot about how you'll enjoy your golden years. But there's a good chance you never thought much about the psychological effect the shelf age might have on you. Retirement often means a loss of identity. Whether you identified as a banker, cook, carpenter, plumber, pastor, or teacher, retirement can cause you to question who you are now that you're no longer working in a structured environment. There are pitfalls to avoid in this new phase.

Worry: Worry is the time we spend fretting about that which usually doesn't happen. The old saying, "Making a mountain out of a molehill," is descriptive of worry.

Dr. Thomas Buzzbee, my physician friend, has a plaque on the wall of his office that states an answer for overcoming worry: "Don't tell God how big your mountain is. Tell the mountain how big your God is." We have a descriptive name for people who worry all the time. They are called worry warts. Don't be one.

As we get off the shelf, we can leave our worries behind. There is a difference between legitimate concerns and useless worry. Fret not!

J. Arthur Rank, an English executive, decided to do all his worrying on one day each week. He chose Wednesdays. When anything happened that gave him anxiety and annoyed his ulcer, he would write it down and put it in his worry box and forget about it until the next Wednesday. The interesting thing was that on the following Wednesday when he opened his worry box, he found that most of the things that had disturbed him the past six days were already settled. It would have been useless to have worried about them. [Source unknown]

The Second 10 Commandments

1. Thou shalt not worry, for worry is the most unproductive of all human activities.

2. Thou shalt not be fearful, for most of the things we fear never come to pass.

3. Thou shalt not cross bridges before you come to them, for no one yet has succeeded in accomplishing this.

4. Thou shalt face each problem as it comes. You can only handle one at a time anyway.

5. Thou shalt not take problems to bed with you, for they make very poor bedfellows.

6. Thou shalt not borrow other people's problems. They can better care for them than you can.

7. Thou shalt not try to re-live yesterday for good or ill, it is forever gone. Concentrate on what is happening in your life and be happy now!

8. Thou shalt be a good listener, for only when you listen do you hear ideas different from your own. It is hard to learn something new when you are talking, and some people do know more than you do.

9. Thou shalt not become "bogged down" by frustration, for 90% of it is rooted in self-pity and can only interfere with positive action.

10. Thou shalt count thy blessings, never overlooking the small ones, for a lot of small blessings add up to a big one.

"There is no favorable wind for the sailor who doesn't know where to go." – [Seneca, I sec. AD]

Loneliness: The world is suffering from a loneliness epidemic. According to a recent survey, nearly half of Americans report sometimes, or always, feeling alone or left out. The same survey revealed one in five people report they rarely or never feel close to people or feel like there are people they can talk to.

Loneliness can sometimes be physical. We may be isolated in our own homes. Some may be confined to a hospital bed, a prison cell, or somewhere far away from loved ones. However, loneliness is not just bound by geography. It is possible to be surrounded by friends, and still, feel desperately lonely. The mind can become its own prison of intruding thoughts, negativity, and anxiety. Who will understand the inward battlefield? We can feel loneliness physically, mentally, emotionally, and even spiritually.

In times when loneliness is felt acutely, we may ask "where are you, God?" "'Why have you forgotten me? Why must I go about mourning, oppressed by the enemy? My bones suffer mortal agony as my foes taunt me, saying to me all day long, 'Where is your God?'" The cry of this psalm (42:9-10) comes from one who feels forgotten and is taunted by others in the midst of their pain "all day long." They are in physical distress, as well as afflicted by the words of those against them.

In times of suffering, loneliness can become more unbearable. Longing for the comfort of others, and especially the presence of God, is achingly apparent. It is important in these times to hold onto the truth that God is sovereign over all, and He indwells believers by His Spirit.

Whatever our outward or inward struggles with loneliness, as difficult as they are, we must cling to the amazing truth that God is with us (Matthew 1:23).

If we begin to doubt the proximity of God to us, it can leave us feeling more cut off than ever before. Yet only one person who ever walked the earth experienced forsakenness from God the Father, and that was Jesus Christ. Jesus cried out to His Father from the cross as His very own bones would have suffered "mortal agony." He cried, ""Eloi, Eloi, lama sabachthani?" (Which means

"My God, my God, why have you forsaken me?")
Matthew 27:46.

It was Christ's forsakenness which enables us to draw near to God today. Equally, it was Jesus who took our sin upon Himself on the cross – the full weight of human sin upon His perfect, sinless flesh. He became like us so we could become like Him. As it says in 2 Corinthians 5:21: "God made him who had no sin to be sin for us, so that in him we might become the righteousness of God."

Some other issues you may face in older years:

- More time and less money. We must structure our life to fit into the new situation.
- A new set of emotions—Oh no, what have I done? What am I going to do now?
- Unstructured days. Create your own structure. If you do not, you will come to the end of the day and wonder where the time went. Make up your mind like you make up your bed – daily. Upon awakening each morning, you can set the tone for the day. I heard Billy Graham say that the first thing he did every morning was to read five Psalms and one chapter from the book of Proverbs. This can be done in a month of mornings. When the month ends, start over and do it again, and again.

I keep a hymn book close by and have a one-person choir. I am certainly no Bev Shea, but I get a great blessing from thumbing thru the hymns. A song in your heart puts a smile on your face. It takes far less effort to smile than to frown.

Make a daily plan and write it on a notepad. A mind in neutral goes nowhere.

Getting back out there

Volunteer: Whether you choose to help out at your church, or the local library or you decide you'd like to volunteer at the hospital, look for ways to get involved in your community. You still have much to offer.

Studies show that seniors who incorporate a low to medium level of volunteering in their life report more satisfaction with life and fewer symptoms of depression than those who didn't volunteer.

Give yourself flexibility to figure it out: You might think that you want to spend your older years painting, cooking, and reading, but then find out that all that time spent at home doesn't fulfill the lifestyle you dreamed about. After 30 years in the workplace, you finally have time to experiment with what you really want.

There are many different ways you can spend your time. And fortunately, there's no need to figure it all out right away. It will likely take a fair amount of experimenting to help you find just the right balance of how you want to spend your time. You can always increase social activities later if you want to stay busier.

The joy of retirement is that you'll have plenty of opportunities to experiment. It's up to you to design the type of day—and kind of life—that you want to live.

Look outward: Reach out to friends. Take the initiative. I endeavor to reach out to at least three friends each day. It is vital to be discreet and not wear out your welcome, but DO IT!

Make room for others. Collaborate with others. Grow your friendships. We need each other Do It – Don't just talk about it. Get with it, do it, now.

Encourage others: Encouraging others is a two-way street. It encourages you when you reach out to encourage someone else.

I make a list of at least three individuals that I want to encourage each day. Reach out and touch someone.

Practice Disciple Stewardship daily: We will be blessed as we reach out and share our time, abilities, resources, and our testimonies daily.

God takes our dedicated little and turns it into a lot.

Evangelism: "That I might "by all means save some." (1 Cor 9:22)

The Apostle Paul had a one-track ministry. It was to bring as many as possible to Jesus and for them to come to know Jesus as their personal Savior. He was willing to do whatever it takes to accomplish this goal.

Charles H. Spurgeon expressed it thus, "To long for the conversion of others makes us Godlike. Do we desire man's welfare? God does so. Would we fain snatch them from the burning? God is daily performing this deed of grace. Can we say that we have no pleasure in the death of him that dieth? Jehovah has declared the like with an oath. Do we weep over sinners? Did not Jehovah's Son weep over them? Do we lay out ourselves for their conversion? Did he not die that they might live? You are made Godlike when this passion for the conversion of others glows within your spirit."

We are at our highest hour when we come off the shelf to pursue immortal souls and introduce them to Jesus. There is no age restriction placed on those who desire to lead others to Jesus. Let us adhere to the following in our quest for souls:

- Get in touch with God. "Be still and know that I am God; I will be exalted among the nations, I will be exalted in the earth." (Psalm 46:10)
- Follow God's Plan. "Trust in the Lord with all your heart and lean not on your own understanding. In all

your ways submit to him and he will make your paths straight. (Proverbs 3:5)

- Be True to God's message. "Then you will know the truth, and the truth will set you free." (John 8:32)

> We've a story to tell to the nations,
> that shall turn their hearts to the right,
> a story of truth and mercy,
> a story of peace and light,
> For the darkness shall turn to dawning,
> and the dawning to noonday bright;
> and Christ's great kingdom shall come on
> earth, the kingdom of love and light.
>
> (From the hymn *We've A Story to Tell to Tell to the Nations.* Colin Sterne)

- Adhere to God's Timing. "Don't you have a saying, 'It's still four months until harvest'? I tell you, open your eyes and look at the fields! They are ripe for harvest." (John 4:35)

Park Cities Church in Dallas, Texas is at the corner of what has been declared to be one of the busiest intersections in the United States. Its massive clock tower is visible from four direction. Two very sobering words," Night Cometh," are inscribed at the bottom of the clock face.

I must work the works of him that sent me, while it is day: the night cometh, when no man can work. (John 9:4)

- Embrace God's Geographical Boundaries. "Go ye therefore, and teach all nations, baptizing them in the name of the Father, and of the Son, and of the Holy Ghost: Teaching them to observe all things whatsoever I have commanded you: and, lo, I am with you always, even unto the end of the world. Amen. (Matt 28:19-20)

The springboard has a landing spot

In the early pages of this book, I mentioned the fact that our memories can serve as a springboard. I referred to my memory springing me to get in touch with Rev A. Oliver Fraser of Ocho Rios, Jamaica. This springboard contact put me in contact with his daughter, Dahlia Fraser. She agreed to write her father's memoirs and put them in a book format. Dahlia is a gifted, trained writer and Bible teacher.

The book," *WHAT A GOD! Reflections of a Centenarian*" by A. Oliver Fraser, has been published and distributed in the Jamaica Baptist Union churches.

I am grateful to the friends who assisted in getting it published.

Working with Dahlia in getting her father's memoirs published has resulted in a genuine friendship. She and

I have established an equal nonprofit partnership called The Well.

We send out a devotional each week by email. Each of us writing on alternate weeks. The list of recipients keeps growing and we have published a first volume of these devotionals. Much to our surprise, the book *The Well Vol. 1* was immediately in great demand especially among older folks who do not use the internet. Copies have been requested for nursing homes and other institutions in America and even internationally. We had no idea that our small ministry would reach such a large audience. God's ways are past finding out. There is no limit to what He can do with what we offer ourselves to Him.

Most recently I have been invited to teach a weekly Bible study on Saturday mornings at the seniors' residence where I live. This opportunity came suddenly after the former teacher was involved in a car accident. It is a joy to me to teach this small group each week and we are all being blessed by it.

To God be the Glory---All of It.

My life verses are Philippians 4:4-7:

"Rejoice in the Lord always; again, I will say, rejoice. Let your reasonableness be known to everyone. The Lord is at hand; do not be anxious about anything, but in everything by prayer and supplication with thanksgiving let your requests be made known to God. And the peace of God, which surpasses all understanding, will guard your hearts and your minds in Christ Jesus."

What a wonderful reminder that Christians should always go to God praising Him and can always go to Him with needs and requests. Especially after the rush of a lifetime of adhering to a super busy schedule, resetting our minds to thank God and go to Him in thankfulness for another day is a great reminder, and seeking the peace of God is a great daily resolution.

Ethel Waters and the Phoenix Crusade

The year was 1966 and I was pastor of a church in Tempe, Arizona. The churches of the area banded together to host The Valley of the Sun Metropolitan Evangelistic Crusade. The meetings were held nightly in The Phoenix Metro Coliseum. Thousands attended. The services were augmented each evening by a Christian celebrity. These included:

Dale Evans – soloist, and screen actress.
Tom Landry, – Coach of the Dallas Cowboys
Jack Williams – Governor of Arizona
Vonda Kay Van Dyke – Miss America
Tom Lester, – actor the TV series "Green Acres."

Miss Ethel Waters – world-famous singer and actress.

A pastor friend went to Los Angeles with me to invite Miss Waters to sing at the crusade. She invited us into her little white bungalow in the heart of the city. Miss Waters said, "O.K. boys. I will be glad to sing about my precious Jesus at your crusade in Phoenix. Let me serve you some tea and cookies. Then, I am going to my piano and give you two precious children an Ethel Waters concert which I will close with "His Eye is on The Sparrow" What a Blessing! I thank God that Ethel Waters came off of the Shelf,

Excerpts from her testimony,

"In 1957, I, Ethel Waters, a 380-pound decrepit old lady, rededicated my life to Jesus Christ, and boy, because He lives, just look at me now. I tell you because He lives; and because my precious child, Billy Graham, gave me the opportunity to stand there, I can thank God for the chance to tell you His eye is on all of us sparrows."

Section 2

Avoiding the Shelf

Ten voices

Richard De Leon

I put myself on the shelf but the Lord took me off. After we retired from the International Mission Board, we went to live in our dream house in the Sangre de Cristo mountains in New Mexico. We had put ourselves on the shelf in our Log Home.

For about 2 years everything was going as planned. We were happy and did limited ministry but most of the time we spent outdoors in our special place. I don't do golf, and for fishing most of the time I just put a weight on the line and if the Lord wants me to catch a fish well, He will have to do a miracle. I just enjoy the outdoors. There are no words to describe the turning of the color on the Aspen trees in those Sangre de Cristo mountains.

We were retired. But the Lord had work for us to do. So, He took us off the shelf.

We left the Sangre de Cristo mountains for East Texas. My wife passed away a couple of years later because her cancer returned. During her treatment, I had the privilege of volunteering in the state prison where I saw the Lord work in a mighty way.

I was also asked to be the Hispanic Coordinator at Green Acres Baptist Church. That was in 2012 and ever since I have been working with Latino Pastors. This is a passion the Lord had placed in my heart. I would like to see hundreds of Latino churches across Texas and why not across the USA? My desire is to assist them in whatever capacity I can, be it training, church planting, retreats at low cost, or just sitting and talking to them and encouraging them. I would like to see these pastors do a mission trip to the Middle East.

In 2021 I left the Hispanic Coordinator position and sold my house to be closer to my 12 grandkids, but I still, have a passion for Latino Pastors. So, I'm still off the shelf.

Thank you, Lord.

Wincie Caskey

We all have one of those high shelves that we need a small step ladder to reach. We usually put items that we don't use often there, like vases, pots and old books. Do you ever feel like God has put you on that shelf and you wonder, "what should I do now?" Upon reaching eighty years old, I'm experiencing that feeling.

I accepted Jesus as my Savior April 1966. For the last twenty-five years I have gone with teams on mission trips to many foreign countries. Most of the time I've been with a team that taught children's workers and church leaders how to present the Gospel using clowns, puppets and mime. Another team I helped with developed women's conferences. After the Covid pandemic, everything has been shut down. I have a friend in Suriname, South America and we text using WhatsApp. We pray for each other, and I hope to someday make a trip to see her again.

For the last twelve years, I have co-taught kindergarteners in Sunday School and loved those five- and six-year-old children. After twenty years at the same church, our pastor retired, and the church made changes that were opposite of what we were used to. It was too much too fast for my husband and me, so we visited other churches in our area. We have found a new church home that includes both types of worship.

There seems to be seasons when the cares of this world distract us from God. My quiet time with the Lord became shorter and shorter and I realized I wasn't hearing His voice as much as I used to. When I read my Bible, my mind was distracted by other things. I began to realize I wasn't as close to the Lord as I used to be and He wasn't the One who moved, it was me! I was disappointed in myself. I wasn't teaching children any longer or doing anything in the new church. I began to feel like I was a piece of pottery sitting on that shelf. When I prayed about it, I would hear, "...lean not on your own understanding; in all your ways acknowledge Him, and He shall direct your paths. (Prov. 3:5-6)

It's time to get back to the basics of Matthew 6:33, "But seek first the kingdom of God and His righteousness, and all these things shall be added to you." The Lord reminded me that Moses was 80 years old when he began his assignment. I've made a choice to let my light shine even if I am that vessel sitting on a shelf, I choose JOY! When I teach art class, I choose joy, when I go to the grocery store, I choose joy. You never know when a smile can lift another person's spirit. Or an act of kindness can brighten someone's day. I realize that God didn't put me on that shelf – I put myself there!

"What does the Lord require of you but to do justly, to love mercy, and to walk humbly with your God." (Micah 6:8b)

Jerry and Erma Kassaw

My friend said, "Jerry, how do you and Erma stay off the shelf ?" Well, several things contribute to that. At 82, I can still hit a golf ball off the tee … not very far, but mostly straight. I solve my sudoku puzzle in the morning paper every day, that is, until the news people raised their rates beyond my limit. So now I don't read their words or work on their puzzles. Erma tends to her backyard birds every day. She calls them her "livestock"!

We have a little tomato patch that keeps us occupied during the spring and summer months. We also team up in the kitchen as Erma is a terrific cook. I'm no chef … I just do the grunt work, like peeling potatoes and chopping onions.

Erma and I are quite a team at sewing and quilting. Erma does the piecing and I assist with the embroidery machine. She is very creative with her crafting of ideas.

There are also our Aggie reunions with 20 to 40 classmates. We have been gathering somewhere in Texas every year for 60 years.

Most importantly, we share a true love for each other. We have been married for 61 years, and now have 3 children, 8 grandchildren, and 3 great-grandchildren. Our shared feelings extend to our love for our Redeemer and Savior, Jesus Christ.

Henry "Butch" Jones

When I retired in April 2009, after spending my entire 42-year business career working for one company, I realized that I was not ready to be placed "on-the-shelf." I am a Chemical Engineer by education but spent the majority of my business life in sales, working for an engineering design and construction company. My clients included oil producers and refiners or engineering contractors located throughout the world.

During my career, I had been relocated 8 times and had lived in Tyler, Texas (my hometown) three times, northern New Jersey (Greater New York City area) twice and the Houston, TX metropolitan area twice. My last 15 years before retirement were spent in Tyler. Carol, my wife of 55 years and I raised 4 kids, two born in New Jersey, one in Tyler and one in Houston. During my business career, I worked with or knew of so-called "workaholics" who had no outside interests, hobbies, etc. After they retired, they had nothing to enjoy. As a result, they became "on-the shelf" and died soon afterwards. Fortunately, I was not one of those types.

I believe that the way to enjoy retirement and, thus, stay "off-the-shelf" involves four steps, as follows:

1. Stay Active: Find your most passionate activities and practice them.

2. Travel: Make and complete a "Bucket List"; visit family and friends.

3. Volunteer: Share your skills, wisdom and experience with the community.

4. Don't Do It: Enjoy, but do not become a slave, to your kids and grandkids.

My passionate activities include playing golf, fishing and watching spectator sports live or on TV. My volunteer activities include Information Desk volunteer at a Heart Hospital, volunteer golf coach for The First Tee youth development organization, Holiday bell-ringer for the Salvation Army, Worship Host and Usher at my church and Asst. Director of my Sunday Morning Bible Study Class at my church. This (SMBS Class) is where I met Frank Gillham. I have also been an active Gideon since my retirement, serving as Camp Chaplain and Camp Secretary.

From my retirement in 2009 until the last half of 2022, I was able to stay "off-the-shelf" and enjoy doing Items 1-4 above. My health (energy and stamina level) declined in the summer of 2022 after having Covid-19 in March. I attributed the symptoms to "long Covid." In November 2022, I was diagnosed with "non-small cell lung cancer." Since late December, I am taking a new cancer medication (one pill) daily and have not had to undergo

radiation or chemotherapy. In essence, I am currently
"on-the-shelf." My Oncologist tells me that the meds are
working. He says that the meds will not "cure" my
cancer but should keep it under control. I suppose that
is the scientific diagnosis and I accept it. Being a
Christian, I know that nothing is impossible for God. I
have many friends that are praying for me to be cured.
My hope is that "Divine Intervention" will cure my
cancer and help me to regain my strength and stamina,
so I can get "off-the-shelf" and back to pursuing the
things I love.

Andy and Marsha Stirratt

We have no intention of being put on the shelf. A few years back we started on a health and wellness journey, not knowing it would turn into a business we would come to love. Now at the ages of 61 and 68, we find ourselves helping others start similar businesses that provide passion and purpose for living. As we age, we have come to realize that we can experience new beginnings every day.

We are also involved and committed to leadership and ministry in our church. Our church believes that life happens in the context of relationships, so we coach and support small-group leaders. In addition, we each lead small groups ourselves.

You could say, between business, church, family, and friends, we are living our best life. Each day we are open to discovering God's purpose for us.

David and Jan Sherrouse

Don't put us on the shelf! David retired in 2004 and Jan retired in 2005. "Retired" to us simply meant not getting up at 5:30 or 6:00 am to go to jobs that we'd been doing for many years. We still had plenty of life ahead of us as we were both in our mid-60s at that time.

Shortly after David retired, he heard about a group of men from our church (GABC) who were called Volunteer Christian Builders. At that time, they were focused on building some "cowboy churches," and had another job lined up to work on a church near Sulphur Springs that summer. Several of the men and their wives, who had travel trailers, pulled their trailers from their homes to the church site and lived in their trailers for the time they were working on the project. We were fortunate enough to have had a travel trailer that we had used for camping the last few years, so we fit right in with this project. I was not retired at this time, but since I was a teacher, I was off for the summer and joined the other wives as "helpers" in that first building project. Cowboy churches were becoming quite popular at that time, and this opportunity was only the first of about four or five churches we helped the VCB build over the next three or four years.

Jan always took her laptop computer along on the building trips because she didn't want to lose her computer skills. She also was busy doing some genealogy work with a group called the "US GenWeb Project" which stayed busy putting information online from various sources so that people all over the country could see records of various counties in the U.S. that were previously only available by going and searching records in person. These records were usually at courthouses, newspaper offices, funeral homes, cemeteries, etc. Since we lived in Texas and most of her involvement centered around her birth county in Georgia, it was always fun to see the names of family members and learn about them without having to travel the 750 miles to do the research in person.

After the church building phase slowed down, David found another interest to keep him busy. This involved transporting cars between car dealers, mainly in Texas, but occasionally in other states. A group of (usually) men would travel together in a minivan to places like Dallas, Houston, Shreveport, etc., and pick up several vehicles that a local dealer had purchased online. They then brought the vehicles back to Tyler to be sold on local car lots. He made lots of friends traveling together with "the guys" and sharing experiences and stories as they traveled. Besides having something to do, he made new friends, and in addition, made a little "mad money" on the side! David enjoyed his driving experiences for about 12-15 years before "retiring" from this adventure in 2021, at the age of 81. He was beginning to tire of driving, especially long distances, and felt he was sometimes not as alert as he should be and did not want to have an accident as some of the "older guys" occasionally did.

When David started his driving phase, Jan continued with her computer work doing a number of different volunteer jobs. The genealogy work went on and she added other things like being the creator and editor of a family newsletter that involved many distant relatives in different states. This family had been having family reunions since 1913 and had yearly reunions in Georgia which Jan and David attended every couple of years. Having two or three newsletters a year helped keep everyone in touch. About seven generations kept the reunions going for over 100 years, but they have begun to have fewer attendees since the younger generations have moved farther away from their roots in north Georgia and have less frequent contact with the other branches. The reunion is still going on as of 2022, but the newsletters have phased out. Jan still hears about and sends out, email notices when there is a death in the family but there are no longer any surviving members of the first three or four generations who were at the earlier reunions.

Jan's newsletters for the family may have ended, but since 2016, she has taken on another volunteer job –

newsletter editor for the Homeowner's Association where they live in Tyler. Each month, she creates a newsletter for the community with the latest updates from the Board of Directors and the property manager, as well as community news (birthdays, social activities, upcoming meetings, maintenance items, etc.) Both Jan and David have done 2-year terms on the Board of Directors for the association. In addition to these jobs, Jan is also the web administrator and keeps our community website updated. This job involved a "learning curve" as our previous administrator resigned suddenly, and someone had to learn quickly how to update and keep the website current and useful for 123 households.

David and Jan are still active members of the Seekers class and of Green Acres Baptist Church. Until the protocol changed because of Covid-19, David was an usher and offering-taker for many years. He also served as an active deacon starting in his late 20s until he elected to become inactive about five years ago. Jan continues to keep the Membership Roster, and records of birthdays, anniversaries, and Care Groups for the Seekers class.

Keeping up with family keeps us as busy as any of the above activities, but as they grow older, the children and grandchildren pick up some of the responsibilities that used to fall on us. First, we were the parents, then the grandparents, and soon we'll be the great-grandparents. We still have things to do, and ways to contribute. I guess that's why we're still here. I guess the Lord will take us while we're still moving instead of picking us up from a place on "the shelf."

Dick Lee

Living in one's nineties may best be described as illustrated in the following: "A couple in their 80s went to the doctor because they were having problems remembering. The doctor's advice was "Write it down." Later that evening, while watching TV the old man got up from his chair and told his wife, "I'm going into the kitchen, do you want anything?" She replied, "Get me a bowl of ice cream, and I would really like some strawberries on top. And you better write it down!" He replied, "No, I can remember that!" The wife then said, "And put some whipped cream on top as well. You should write that down or you will forget!" To which the old man retorted, "For goodness' sake, leave me alone – ice cream, strawberries, and whipped cream. Got it!" Twenty minutes later he stumbles out of the kitchen and hands his wife a plate of bacon and eggs. She stares at the plate for a few minutes and says, "You forgot my toast!"

Having lived for 92 years, and some months, I can attest to the inability to remember names, places, and often just simple words. Since turning 85 it has become much more difficult to tell a story coherently, without stumbling over words I have used effectively for many years. Many times, a day I will go from one room to another and when I get there have to stop and think why am I here?

May I hasten to add that I feel very blessed compared to others with whom I come in contact, some much younger? As we grow older we need to stay active and exercise. For many years I walked 3 miles a day, but for the last 2-3 years I have had to curtail that distance. When I say remain active it also includes maintaining social contacts and using God-given talents effectively. In other words, "Don't set your buckets down and do nothing!" Stay involved. Of course, it becomes more difficult with each passing day, and one often feels like saying, "just leave me alone and let me wallow in my misery and forgetfulness." But the key to survival is staying involved.

What else is involved when you reach elderly status? Well, for one thing, you start to lose control. Children become much more involved and begin to give advice on what you should do. Personally, I have not experienced that yet because I gave fair warning to leave us alone on where we live and where we drive, and how far we go. Our youngest daughter has said to her sister, "You will have to take Dad's car keys because I'm not!" My response was "No one takes my car keys until I am ready to give them up"!

I rejoice in the Lord that he has given me all these years to enjoy and be fruitful. Getting older tends to bring on grumpiness and complaints, and at my age, I certainly have plenty of that. However, in my heart, I want to be more Christ-like. My hope and prayer are to live in the Spirit, manifesting the Fruit of the Spirit, which is Love, Joy, Peace, Patience, Goodness, Kindness, Faithfulness, Gentleness, and Self Control. If we live as God intended us to live, then what age we are has no significance. Moses was 80 when God called him to deliver His people from bondage in Egypt. Certainly, we have plenty of aches and pains, and we lose our ability to think clearly. We become forgetful and often lose our incentive to keep active and involved. But God is good and will sustain us even through our old age. My new mantra is "keep the old man out...just don't let him in!"

Dennis Ortega

I have volunteered with Gideon's International for several years. I am being kept off the shelf by my speaking schedule for the Gideons. Everywhere I go people want to hear the famous story of how a Gideon New Testament presented to a depressed Japanese man changed his life and the amazing events that followed. Here is the story:

Soon after World War II ended, during the Allied occupation of Japan, and during the middle of the evening sermon at the Mitaka Baptist Church in the suburbs of Tokyo, a neatly dressed man, a former Japanese military officer, stood up and asked if he could speak. It was highly unusual for someone to break into a sermon but since this gentleman had never attended a church service before he did not know. Those in attendance were amazed at what he had to say. He declared, "*My name is Inuyama. I was previously married to a very unhappy wife. We seldom conversed and were often rude to each other. We remained married for the sake of our honor.* (This is very important in Japanese culture.)

Then I noticed a change. Finally, she confided in me that the change was because of a new Friend that she had invited into her life. In disbelief, I wondered who this could be. She said His name is Jesus and that she met him at the Mitaka Baptist Church."

Then, Mr. Inuyama said, *"If Mr. Jesus is here tonight, I really would like to meet Him. Perhaps He could change my life in the same way he did my cherished wife."*

By this time, Mrs. Inuyama, who was seated near the front of the church and had been totally unaware of her husband's presence, turned in disbelief, got up, went to him, bowed lowly and stood by his side.

Mr. Inuyama met Mr. Jesus that night! About three months later, after a period of indoctrination, my friend and brother, Frank Gillham, who was the young missionary pastor of that church, had the distinct pleasure of baptizing Mr. Inuyama.

Bro. Gillham distinctly remembers that three months prior to that interrupted evening service; the women of the church were meeting on a Thursday morning for their weekly Bible study. Mrs. Hirano was leading the Bible study.

She paused and said, *"As I look around the room, I note that every person here is a believer and a follower of Jesus Christ. You ladies pray while I go out into the street and find someone that we can share our faith with."* She did just that. Guess who she encountered. It was Mrs.

Inuyama. She had been to the vegetable market and was returning home.

Mrs. Hirano invited her to join the meeting. A bewildered Mrs. Inuyama accepted the invitation and, for the first time ever, heard the message of eternal salvation in Jesus Christ. A few weeks later, she accepted Christ as her savior and began to attend church regularly.

Mrs. Inuyama's husband was very suspicious of these meetings that she attended on Sundays. He required her to meet a "white glove inspection" standard before he would allow her to leave the house and attend church. Never would she imagine that her husband would one day walk into the Sunday evening service and ask to meet Mr. Jesus.

But the story is even more remarkable. The conversion of the Inuyamas was just part of the ripple effect of another remarkable event that took place years earlier.

Mrs. Hirano, the Bible study leader who invited Mrs. Inuyama to the group, was the wife of Dr. Shiro Hirano. Shiro Hirano was a young man when the Allied Forces, under General Douglas MacArthur were occupying Japan. Japan had lost the war. They were a country in the shame of defeat. Many of the best men felt that their honor had been forever lost and committed suicide.

Shiro Hirano, a budding young scientist, decided to join the hundreds of others who were taking their own lives. The most common way to do it was to book passage on a boat. Take the family's treasured, symbolic sword, sail out into the ocean about ten miles from the shore, take the sword and disembowel themselves as they were jumping into the ocean waters.

The Hiranos' little five-year-old daughter sensed that something was severely wrong. She, in desperation, clung to her father and begged him not to go away. Shiro decided that he would postpone his fatal journey by one day. It was a beautiful spring day in Tokyo. Mr. and Mrs. Hirano and their little girl were sitting on the porch of their small home when they noticed some Allied soldiers of the occupying forces approaching. Mr. Hirano, in fear, tried to shield his little family from these perceived barbarians. As he was attempting to leave the scene, one of the young soldiers, a lad from Canada, shouted and got his attention and told him he wanted to talk with him. Shiro understood a fair amount of English and was captivated by the young soldier's smile. They chatted for a long time and the young soldier told Shiro that he would like to introduce him to his best friend, His name was Mr. Jesus. The Holy Spirit touched Shiro's heart and he invited Jesus into his life. He quickly ran to the harbor and cancelled his fateful passage on the Hara Kiri ship. Just before the young Canadian soldier left, he said. *"By the way, I want to give you a gift. It will help you to know much more about your new-found friend, Mr. Jesus."* With that, he handed him a copy of a Gideon New Testament.

They never saw each other again, but Shiro confided in Bro. Gillham that he was eagerly waiting to meet the young Canadian lad in heaven and thank him for introducing him to Mr. Jesus and for the copy of the Word that literally changed his life.

Shiro Hirano went on to become Dr. Shiro Hirano, a Professor of Chemistry in one of Japan's leading universities and board chairman of the Lion Dentifrice Corporation. He and his lovely wife evolved as national leaders in Christianity in Japan.

And what became of Mr. Inuyama? He now serves as a deacon in Mitaka Baptist Church, the same church where years ago he had boldly interrupted the sermon asking to meet Mr. Jesus.

Note the sequence of events in this remarkable true story:

1. Japan is defeated in World War 2 and surrenders.

2. Soldiers from the USA and Canada occupy Japan.

3. Many young Japanese men commit suicide because they believe they have lost their honor.

4. Shiro Hirano, a young scientist, books passage on a suicide ship.

5. Delays one day at insistence of his small daughter.

6. A Canadian soldier visits with him and introduces him to Jesus and gives him a Gideon New Testament. He accepts Christ as his Savior and leads his wife to do the same. They become members of the Mitaka Baptist Church.

7. Mrs. Hirano leads the women of the church in a Thursday Morning Bible Study.

8. She invites a passerby, Mrs. Inuyama, to attend the session. Mrs Inuyama receives Jesus and starts attending church.

9. Mr. Inuyama notes the distinct difference in his wife, and she tells him that the difference is because she has met and accepted Jesus as her Savior.

10. Mr. Inuyama visits her church and asks to meet Jesus.

Let us be reminded what Isaiah 55:11 says:

*"So shall my word be that goes forth out of my mouth,
It shall not return unto me void,
But it shall accomplish that which I please,
And it shall prosper in the things whereto I sent it."*

Debbie Stewart

I am in my seventeenth year as a public school bus driver. It is my privilege to meet these children both early in the morning as they are beginning their day and, in the afternoon, when they are returning home. This gives me the opportunity to encourage them. I try to make their ride to school each day a cheerful experience.

I am also in my seventh year as the driver of the shuttle bus for my church. I transport senior church members from the car parking lot to the front entry of the church and back to their car when the church service is over. This is a cherished blessing.

I live in the country near Rockwall. My late husband and I built our home forty-one years ago and I still live there. My son lives nearby and that is comforting.

I am seventy-one years old and still working. I have no desire to be placed on the shelf and it is my intention to stay off of The Shelf

Chuck Doyle

Staying off the shelf can be summed up in three words—
Endure, Endure, Endure. Stay engaged daily with your
family, your church and your community. Don't
quit. God is in charge. Stay Engaged.

Epilogue

ONWARD!

God Commands, we must follow. God is our leader.

Wherever He Leads I will Go!

I have heard the voice of Jesus telling me still to fight on. He promised never to leave me. Never to leave me alone.

You see, it is impossible to be alone if you know our Lord Jesus.

I hope this booklet will encourage you to make an inventory of your capabilities. and continue to use them for the good of mankind and the glory of God.

We live in a challenging world. And regardless of our age, we can make a contribution that will make the world better. Do it. Don't quit. Keep on keeping on. Age is not a matter with God. Our challenge: To dedicate ourselves and whatever time God gives us to serve Him and to serve other people.

With God's help, we can make our world a better place in which to live.

Bruce Bruinsma shared some interesting statistics in his book *The Retirement Reformation,* that show how we can accelerate God's mission to reach the ends of the earth!

- More than 10,000 North Americans turn 65 every single day.
- Of those 10,000 - roughly 4,000 of them are Christ-followers.
- Retirement once lasted only a few years, but now lasts approximately 30 years - the same amount of time as prime working years between ages 20 and 50.
- There will be 32 million church members over 65 in the next 10 years.

So, what does this mean? It means that there is a MAJOR UNTAPPED ARMY of retired men and women God wants to unleash for His glory in the nations!!!